811.54   c.1
C585

Clair, Maxine
  Coping with gravity: poems

COLLEGE OF THE SEQUOIAS
LIBRARY

DISCARDED

DEMCO

COPING WITH GRAVITY

COPING WITH GRAVITY

poems by maxine clair

COLLEGE OF THE SEQUOIAS
LIBRARY

Some of these poems have appeared, sometimes in different versions, in the following publications:

Gargoyle: "Reincarnation"; *The Washington Review of the Arts:* "Lust," and "For Jesse Who Froze To Death"; *Nethula Journal:* "Reincarnation"; *Whose Woods These Are:* "Sunday"; *Obsidian:* "Daughter," "Running," "Flying Africans," "The Other Lady"; *Primavera:* "Lone Lily Beside the Road"; *Evidence of Community:* "Naptime"; *Cooke Poetry Anthology:* "Harriet Tubman Said. . ."; *Folio:* "When Exactly Is the Eleventh Hour Past?," "Rosedale, Kansas," "After Ever After"; *GHA Letter:* "Moonlighting."

I wish to thank Ann Darr and Katherin Mattern for time, energy, advice, and handholding during the production of this book.

Library of Congress Cataloging-in-Publication Data

Clair, Maxine, 1939-
    Coping with gravity.

    I. Title.
PS3553.L2225C67   1988   811′   87-37162
ISBN 0-931846-32-3

WASHINGTON WRITERS' PUBLISHING HOUSE
P.O. Box 15271
Washington, DC 20003

For Stephen, Michael, Joey, Adrienne

○ Contents

I. Coal Oil and Sugar

○ Rosedale, Kansas

Mirages hovered above undulant highways
and summer stomped his dusty feet,
conjured up sunflowers
that ran wildly through fields of cornsilk.
Giant brown faces with yellow rays
stampeded to pavement edge
and stood cooling their feet in the clay.

Blue racers that slept between slats
of a swinging bridge became Python.
Roused by Amazon and Watusi
they slithered to a rocky cathedral
in the creek bed,
and choirs of cicada droned a fugue
of The Seven-Fold Amen.

When the moon like new silver
rolled on edge across black velvet,
Orion laid down his shield
to play hide-and-seek with lightning bugs.
Children caught his eyes in mason jars,
kept the stars to hold to
and went to seek their fortunes.

○ Lone Lily Beside the Road

Lilium superbum
Stem—three to seven feet
Flower—orange to scarlett

It must have been a city wind came
rasping through seams in sleep's
window, calling her name, telling
her to kiss the face that rose in the pyre
of years raked to a pile and lit,
                                        kiss the face
of the old woman who taught the old religions:
Cleaning, Cooking, Washing.
Watching the starch pot boil
once-upon-June days, waiting
to pour bluing in, Mae Pearl
talked about dyeing her hair, never
talked of leaving, never said she wanted
cities that hummed, just flipped
to that chapter, ripped out her life
and was gone
                to the dogs,
to better days, a postmark, a thin circle around
a snapshot, red-headed woman.
Gone to hell. Gone to Jesus.

Now her amazed tongue
sang resurrection, a homing
song, and when those summers rushed
to greet her like great aunts
claiming their own, home hit

irretrievable as the wrinkled
face gone, and the sagging
jaws of house and barn—

all smoothed, paved flat
into a curve of I-35
                    where she stands
a wild, flaming sultriness among witnesses,
the enduring weeds. In their reedy
throats they whisper,
Where you gonna run to?

○ Coal Oil and Sugar, 1954

When the nine o'clock whistle blows
our way, we can smell manure and bacon
from the packing house across the river.
The August night sky leans down for us
to touch. Mamma Hayes braids her hair

on her porch. Down the block somebody
yells, *All hid?* Next door Georgie, who's
too slow to read and cannot go to school, begs to stay
outside until ten when the street light goes out
and we go to bed thinking of school one sleep away.

Attucks, Wheatley, Douglass—mostly names
of schools we know, Dunbar Annex is ours,
a haven on the second floor of the Agency
where official workers must not be disturbed.
Hear our verses opening the day, reluctantly

at first, *God is love. Make a joyful noise. . .*
See us reciting in single file, eight rows
of faces, brown and artless as sunflowers:
  Between the dark and the daylight,
  When the night is beginning to lower,

our skinny stalks rooted to this soil
of English, arithmetic, geography.
We lift our voices and sing—not the dirges
yet, not the curses we will learn before
we sing love songs again. Black still verges

on the profane, the color of a bad word for female
dogs; for weapons, loaded snowballs in February,
on our sleds all day, a dose of coal oil and sugar
down our throats to ward off whooping cough. With
pudding and juniper tea our evenings boil over

like the pot on the back burner whose steam
rises and stains the wallpaper in shapes we dream
about. We cannot know that when we turn this page,
a schoolboy face with a bullet hole, the murdered
face of Emmet Till, will fill those shapes.

The smooth, tied hands with mud from the bottom
of the river will worry our dreams like blood
on snow. We lift our voices and sing. Negro
History Week and we have forgotten the second
stanza but not our catechism. We know

the list: Ira Aldridge, Marian Anderson, Benjamin
Banneker, Ralph Bunche, George Washington Carver,
W.E.B. DuBois, Duke Ellington, Marcus Garvey
and on. Twenty-five Negro Leaders. We cut their
mythical figures from the glossy pages of *Ebony*

where they tell us to learn all we can, be twice
as bright. We ignore this reading lesson.
Those Negroes are history. They can bring
nothing from yesterday. We are today. In the only
future we can see, we are sliding downhill into spring.

○ Penmanship

Cursive writing separated us
from the little kids that year,
promised us we would be flourishes
of gold ink on a white bond expanse
of future. Letters flowed into
one another like jacks, bangs, secrets,
and banana caramels, spelling out
girlfriends.

Then Norma's mother died:
draped in a navy blue sheet,
put into a Black Maria,
lowered into a hole.
We went away searching
for Norma's mistake, one something
more fleeting than Orpheus' backward
glance that set this thing in motion.

We sensed it then. Like a teacher
with the final word it would stand
stark, guiding our lives
as we made ovals, strokes, loops,
and slants, each of us outlining
one unknowable letter
in the endless alphabet.

○ Harriet Tubman Said. . .

There are many kinds of being scared:
hiding out with snakes in a swamp,
praying in a whisper so low the Lord
strains to hear. And in morning light
all gold and flashy, you trample down
marshweed beside the road, shivering at
every bird call, or you hold on
to some long, way back love, wishing
against all odds your name will come up
on his lips. Sometimes it's a brief glimpse
of old square-toed death, reared-up
on his hind legs, waiting.

My train only moves one way and it's up
a mountain. You left fear standing
in a field with a whip. He was your
running start. Now he's sniffing around,
licking your heels, tasting your sweat.
You turn and I see him behind your eyes.
He suits you fine 'cause he's all you had
for so long. But I'll tell you this,
you can't go back. Fear will never be
so close to you as this cold iron finger
I hold in your ear. You can only die once.
You can die now, or you can be free.

○ Superstar

Our own Ms. Magenta
bleeds into our presence
wound tightly round a crescent
of white teeth that chop life
into tidbits, served up on party
trays, don't you know.

She runs her lines
projecting through our psyches:
money-market, fortune telling,
behavioral adjustment, best
designer—bathroom, den, and flatware.

She baits us with her cues,
finagles us to corners
with her blocking,
ad libs it while she's on.

(We're on).
The room is dark
except for a slice of light
obliquely falling.
Magenta steps to catch it,
balances its beam across
her shoulders. Her act is over.
Magenta takes the stage.

○ The Folly of Power

In preparation for a war that might come
planes practiced maneuvers
over the airfield a mile from our house.

On winter afternoons
I could hear their buzzing,
not at all muted by the snow.
I watched their corkscrew dives
in July when throbbing panes
of heat rose from the pavement.
I nurtured one desire, steady
as their drone, to see just one
of those skimmers fail.

Finally
I saw it, the skimmer, zooming
my way, losing perspective,
missing the sign on top of the hotel
the steeple almost too tall.
It roared overhead, sliced
through the sky like a silver
zipper laying bare in my brain
a hard, bitter plum.

When the noise faded in with blaze
and debris, I climbed on my bike
and headed toward the smoke.

○ Martin Luther King

A sermon
in earth tones
breathed out from the lungs
of a people.

A spirit
quick and transparent,
dancing on mountaintops
at midnight, taunting
the sun to wake on up.

○ Flying Africans

Solomon done fly, Solomon done gone/
Solomon cut across the sky, Solomon gone home!
— *Song of Solomon*   Toni Morrison

Countless souls—
stolen from their warmth
to wander in shackled bodies
and die in foreign cold—
have journeyed back
across waters, to rest.

Fictitious black heroes
have flown, taken off,
dropping their babies
in mid-air,
leaving their women
to mourn and grieve.

I am the son, fallen
to earth, the seed
of their dreams, the blues.
When the eagle flies, I fly
on dust from the angels
at 18th and Swann.

One of these nights
when the moon has climbed
half the sky,
into its light a silhouette
of wings will curve the wind
to its advantage, a purple sheen

will flash, a giant bird
will swoop into blackness.
It will be me.

○ The Other Lady

I smelled the sharp sickly-sweet odor
of the cocaine. . . Then tiny prickly feet
of ecstasy started dancing through me. . . I
felt a superman's surge of power.
        —"Iceberg Slim," *Pimp. The Story of My Life*

What can a simple woman
offer? She holds you
like the moon holds night
around it to flaunt its light,
masquerading as a star.

Anymore you're never free,
based on how you could be
living without her: dealing
with your real rages, letting
my real fingers translate love.

But you and this good-time girl
work it all out to be a boogie,
a freak tango, the slide.
She won't relent until she's locked
in your brain in a lowdown slow drag.

○ The Adulterers

In the first place
don't mess with no Pharisee men.
They don't mind taking your time,
but they treat you back-street.

Before they picked up stones,
threatening my life trying to make
a point, sleeping with another
woman's man wasn't really no thing,
more like a little story to spruce up
the big one, but never a real
climax, know what I mean?

I said vows.
They said vows, too. We never
hurt nobody so I was too through
when this gang of priests and elders
—Pharisees mind you—come hauling
me out early in the morning
just for sleeping with a woman's
husband while she was off

in the valley. They grabbed
me round my neck, threw me
out in the raod, tore my new
wine-colored robe with the silver
threads around the hem. I would
have fought them if it wasn't
for the Man they brought me to.

He was squatting in the dust
and they called out to Him. Sounds
to me like they trying to catch Him
in a lie about being a teacher
and all. By now they picking up
stones and asking Him what he knows
about Moses' law that says
I'm supposed to die.

Well now, this Teacher stands up
and the sun's bouncing off Him
like gold pieces and He looks at me.
Let me tell you, I know when a man
wants me and let me tell you
He didn't. And He didn't pity
me either, He wasn't even lording

it over me. He just looked.
And way back deep in His eyes,
seem like I could see a kind
of thing that the love I been
having couldn't touch. Looking
at Him was like falling
in the sea and the longer I looked
I could see He don't speak nothing

but pure truth and it got me
thinking about vows and such.
Like: they different from words,

they real, alive. Must be living
truth. If that's so, when a man
and woman vow it, they can get the same
feeling between them as a mother and child,

and as two brothers all at the same time
'cause they choose it and if that's so,
when they say I do, they talking about
a whole life thing that don't
get broken just from sleeping
with someone else. But nobody in their
right mind would want to come
between that kind of feeling anyway.

It would be an empty thing,
like hollering in a cave with no
echo—nothing you send comes back,
you can't get no real connection.
I was looking in the eyes
of this Man and I was making
a whole lot of sense to myself.

Well the Teacher Man looks
at these Pharisees and asks if any
of them ever done anything wrong
like lie or steal or call somebody
out of their name or swear or cheat
or gossip. Of course nobody
can say nothing. Then said this
Teacher, *Whoever is without*

the tiniest bit of sin can throw
the first stone at this woman,
talking about me. By then I
wasn't even scared. They all
tucked tail and slinked off.
And then He says to me, *Go*
and I went.

Since then I ain't had nothing
to do with nothing that wasn't truth,
especially no Pharisees.

○ When Exactly Is the Eleventh Hour Past?

Lately, after midnight, when the house is cold
and I can smell it rusting, I look into
a blackened sky—shooting stars that once
were charms merely hiss and fall.

We sit around a scarred table
and cover it with proper words, stilted lace.
We measure days by the number of times
our eyes meet and hold.

Once we had time
but time pulls through fast now,
out of control, no knots to grab.
It burns.
Our calluses are gone,
we're down to flesh.

○ Coping With Gravity

"Heated discussions" scare me.
I shouldn't worry, a little faith
and things work out—a hard rain clears
the hot night's muddled breath,
an unwanted dream flinches
in a glimmering rush
from the sun.

This morning the elevator takes me in.
I go with it, avoiding eyes, enduring
moments outside of gravity. We stop.
A woman in pink hurries toward the door,
closing, and sticks in an arm, risking
everything.

Seven, six, five—each light flashes as we
move—and we'll get to four, I know it
as I know you'll bring home a new wine
tonight. See how the past becomes
the future!

Still, with these subtle creaks, sluggish
doors, I think of failures going
unnoticed like glances losing warmth
by degrees.

And speeding down this shaft this morning
I am struck by the imperceptible
difference between riding
and falling.

○ Blank

Mornings, even before the dream-fog lifts,
it starts. I wake to the sound of memory
idling in my head, waiting to rattle off
the day's indictment: no poems.
It nags like hunger and I am the cook.
In my mind, my house of invisible rooms,
I shuttle between will and feeling.
Notice how they echo my predicament:
will/ a single committed syllable;
feeling/ an impression, but where
to from here?

On the street I step one-two-one-two,
avoiding the cracks, chanting this cadence
of time-tables when time meant to multiply
and I could count on being warned of dead-
lines ahead. I count the windows
of a building ahead, something to do, my mind like a jogger
running in place at the stop light.

A siren blares and I recall
how I never could figure why ambulance
is written in reverse across the front
of the vans. Then how one day, without
thinking, I suddenly knew. I could not
name this improbable sense that slips
things to me like a smuggler: the image
of a blind man feeling for a window,
a word read backwards in the mirror.

I should be turning a corner here, instead
I make lists, wordgames based on the premise
and best fantasy of all: everything can
be learned, broken down to easy units
like steps of an intricate dance.
And isn't this a dance I'm doing,
waking, straining, winding down,
step-shuffle-step, trying to find
by rote what I already know by heart?

II. Deja Vu

○ Winter

I like winter
not for the way moisture rearranges itself
into lace on the slick bark of cherry
trees, nor the odd mix of odor and aroma
(cabbage and nutmeg) that hangs in the house,
nor my arms' lust for flannel. But by November
when the earth is in reverie, I remember
how old folks took inventory of what

they had to work with—so many
slabs of bacon, cords of wood,
jars of pears—and I like the thin
ice of need that turns water to soup, stone
to pillow and for a little warmth, doesn't
count on a lover who comes around
as briefly as winter sun.

I like winter earth in REM sleep: sprouting
roots like a great neural storm, winds
breathing rapidly, sifting through elements
for the millionth time to come up with a new
spring. I like eventuality in quiescent things—
nitrogen, carbon, a cell, a dream.

○ For Jesse Who Froze To Death

Winter's a hard core Big Mamma, Jesse.
We've seen her snowflakes
stripping their lace,
throwing their bodies down
with no grace,

yes, we know her.
Her winds scour city corners
spoiling for a rumble.
She's a junkie, Jesse,
her stuff's uncut,

she'll steal your life
if you nod. She wants
to be your woman, loves
a desperate man. We placed
our bets and dressed you

for the wedding.

○ Momma Has Come a Thousand Miles To See Me

She used to be filled with mornings,
a cinnamon girl with good
hair, chasing goats down Mission Road.

Now she's on an excursion flight—
across circuitboard cities, straight-
drop ridges, drab valleys—
cruising over the patchwork
the way the spirit hovers
above the body near the end.

Out there she still can be
Althea Gibson, sweating, brilliant
in the sun, smashing what's bound
to be an ace serve,

or Carmen McRae singing,
"Long Before I Knew You,"
in a familiar alto,
familiar stubby fingers
backing herself up
on piano.

When I see her at the airport,
I see a silver thread tightening:
dreams folded away like old
negligees, eyes lit

from the back, hair
in frost-gray waves. I glimpse
the first long night we lived
as one and hug that night,
my arms flimsy from swinging
long and free.

○ Dear Daughter

You've got these years
to make into a quilt,
scraps of satin and muslin
must be fitted together
side-by-side.
Your fingers may sweat
as you sew on the lining,
but the salt will last
far into winter.

It's like this, Momma;
You've got these years
to eat up. Boil and honey them
like cranberries. If you let them
they string together,
each no different
from the one before.
Then they dry brittle,
their bitterness difficult
to swallow.

○ The Marriage

My mother made
it clear—
in those days
she was green,
big for her age,
a spring chicken,
and what did she get?
Pregnant,
a mother who said,
or else, a railroad-
yard worker, a room
in his father's house,
a pint of orange sherbet,
two magazines.

My father never
told us what he got.

○ Sunday

there were times she would play the piano
she would throw back her head and her wavy black hair would
dangle
she would strike the chords and move on the piano stool
and sing
Lord Jesus can I have a talk with you
Lord Jesus won't be long till I'll be through
and tears would be streaming down puffy rust cheeks
if there is no God there ought to be
the way she played and cried

○ Farsighted

Nature has overwhelmed me
with small print and begun
calling in her loans.
The opthalmologist says
the eyes are first to surrender.
He becomes judge and prosecutor
dragging you, my eyes, into court
to show cause why I should
honor you at this failing.

With his green squares, red
lines, his unyielding parade:
     D O T F B 8 A H
he makes me stumble and err,
repeatedly, until I admit I, too,
am duped. He shows me the spare
eyes he has made for himself
for reading coarse, reading fine,
scope work and art galleries.

He chides me when I tell him
about the wisdom of organs,
each cell and its own intelligence;
about how relative perfection is,
and how this blur I've come
to live with feels cozy
as the song I've always sung
with made-up words, even though
I've heard the real ones.

Despite his insistence
that you, my eyes, are going,
much more than hints of light
remain. Your loss of power
to change focus may be my clue
to shift from what has gone
wrong here to what lies—
so compelling—in the distance.

○ The Kansas City Call Weekly

A day unfolds, a little chit
of time, plotting to be remembered.

He should be innocent, he lived a block
away, part of our gang, the only one
who had money for pickles or doughnuts
when we went home lunchtimes through
the hollow, in the muddy spring.

They quote his mother. She says
he'd never take a life. Once
his snowball put out an eye,
a rock inside, an accident.
He made good grades, we moved away

and maybe he stopped going
to the Baptist church or loved
someone who didn't love him back
or had the special moment of madness
each of us is slated for.

How ordinary the things
we fold and toss away in discarded
days, days that convene and hang
in our minds like booms swinging
toward an old building.

○ Saturday Night Jam

The high priest Tito commands
the booth—elevated pulpit
glowing through the smoke—
where three turntables spin
above tiny pulsing lights,
candles on his altar.
With flicks of his wrists
he splits, mixes, amplifies
the meter, sends it on down
like a flinty sermon
to the dance floor. It solders
soul to solar plexus, makes brown bodies
rock and sweat, hammer the air
in amen.

○ Lust

You creeping noctural pest.
I've come to know your cruising gray coat
and scurf-like tail
but will I set the traps?

This night you come albino,
pink and white, tender pure amor.
Shall we both pretend?

Hot breath sniffs my cornerstone,
a monogamous rock that hardly hides its cracks.
Insistent paws scratch at windows
opaque with promises I etched inside.
Those rodent teeth gnaw at loins
of proud oak and sweet pine
that needn't be reduced to ordinary sawdust.

Come round to my back door, ole Lust,
I'll let you in this time.

○ After Ever After

"The servants complain
that your kindness is rotting
with acrid fumes. For three nights
they have seen you kneeling at the fireplace,
picking through ashes, calling to fairies
and your dead mother,

                    what is it?
Haven't I loved you well?
Your father and his family are in exile,
I've burned the slippers, melted them away,
given you a castle separate from mine
and your own account,

yet you go around
in that gray denim sack and your hair. . .
I have asked the physicians
to lift your face—the lines
are pulling down, down
and your smile is etched.
Royalty must wear well, Ella dear."

○ Friday

A thin, red wand glides round,
touching time every fifth second.
A discreet thermostat almost clicks,
embarrassed for recycling the air.
Brittle promises stand erect
then crumble on the heap.
The crowded needs push
to the margin, push
till the bell rings.

○ Moonlighting

Alert until midnight
my right brain languishes
in my left brain's perfect discipline.
Sleep waits like a patient lover
biding his time.
I hurry through the vacant city
racing other stragglers,
every intersection blinks
caution at us. We work two jobs,
a whole life costs.

A red light holds us
in the moment, we tap out
golden oldies (In the Still
of the Night). Behind me
in his new car,
part of a couple doubles
the effort to get further faster,
blows his new horn
as caution returns
like a monotonous busy signal.

Outside the city
night opens clean,
its stars busy
on the graveyard shift. When I swing
into the winding shadow
of my street, I can see half

the moon rising late, hanging
off kilter, loitering
as if the other half
could catch up.

○ Running

Cafe curtains top the list:
Keep out, family inside
that plans to stay
for longer than the end
of the month,

but curtains stay at the top
of the list, ahead of
shoes, bicycles,
a new iron, an all-you-can-
eat shrimp dinner

for you and the three
of them asleep down the hall
knowing that when
they wake you'll be
making cereal and lunches

and you're awake
with a glass of chablis
and two puffs off the joint
your friend rolled for you
to have for this night

when you will dream
of a river
to cross, rushing,
muddy water,
a baby aloft

over your head
using up your arms
so that you can't swim
and you go down once,
go down twice. . .

and this is one of those
going down dreams
that return like checks
marked insufficient funds
before payday, before Saturday

night when you have twelve hours
to come off being Mom,
the willing-worker-who's
-never-on-time, the not-bad-
looking-single-lady

in a who-do-you-think-
you-are neighborhood of doubles:
husband and wife, two jobs, two cars,
two children, two bikes,
two aunts who can come,

two bodies warming each other
for years (can I get a witness?)
and you have twelve hours
in a model condo with his
classical and jazz,

California wines, well-
appointed body, and your
unconnected fantasies of how
next time when you reach
dry land you will run.

○ May A.M.

You wake one morning and the sun
is grinning. Trees have erupted
in the night, spilling sap
promiscuously; buds sprout
from cracks in winter-white rocks,
everything chlorophyll infected.

This is not respect. Some
of us find comfort in smooth,
clean trees, every crooked
finger apparent. We need
ceilings, gray skies to push beyond.

But this enchantment comes on
like soft pornography, all red
cheeks and honeysuckle, teasing
us into believing it could last.

○ Naptime

Take heart from the little ceremonies:
She sits in the middle of a high-up bed
clinging to discovery and crackers
and every afternoon something comes to pester her.
It approaches in stealth—she falls back
and wails, offended not afraid.
It stings her eyes, she mashes them
with soft, balled fists
and when tears won't cool the sting
she folds arm under arm and rolls
to force it from the bed.
It spreads further than she can reach.
She gathers what she can of it to her chest,
and holds it down with a fretting
that is mostly song; and she rocks,
satisfied that each minute delayed is gain.
As she reviews her strategy
the bars come down one eyelash at a time
and she flies away.

○ Daughter At Ten

Plaited down, snaggle-toothed,
fragile mahogany sapling,
bartering with a Double-Dutch wind:
Jump eenie, meenie, goos-a-leeni
oo bump bump-a-leenie. . .

Sprouting blossoms that dress your nimble sprigs,
stretching to a lean, strong trunk
that will not shrink or swell or warp,
a veneer for the lesser woods:
Take a peach, take a plum,
take a stick, of bubble gum. . .

Yearning for the coming rustle
of your broad-leafed skirts in the wind,
it comes, Baby Girl, it comes:
If you want it you can take it,
do the Alabama shake it,
change ten-twenty-thirty-forty-fifty. . .

○ What Mother Doesn't Cook?

You would think
I'd be tired of the heat
that sits in the kitchen
like August in the city,
but I am a runner losing
count of the laps and the track
goes on, twisting.
Eyes that took in my songs,
my warnings, have gone stark,
looking at me level,
spelling out a brandnew version
of how it is.

With the first case of colic
you disprove the myth that fitness
is intrinsic and you're
tentative, a Sunday jogger thinking
of Jim Fixx and Arthur Ashe, athletes
whose hearts ran short. It could
happen. You could fail. For an endless
somersault of night after day
after night you watch for cracks
that could swallow your chance
to rectify what's past by shaping
up the future.

And you go on, you manage, you hit
your stride, you move to automatic
where you, too, stand stirring
a pot no one will taste, sweating

in the heat long past the time
when you ran lanes of mothering
with eyes closed,
limbs up and out like precision
scissors, sun riding your shoulders,
the wind a tympany in your ears, when
your heart's lubb-dupp percussion would not quit.

○ Empty Nest Syndrome

When it had rained forty days
and forty nights, when water
covered the earth for five months,
and Noah was 600 years old,
he sent out a dove that come
back with an olive branch
cooing, *Land ho!*

And Noah knew then
that the very boat
he had made from resinwood,
the boards he had tightened
with fiber and covered with pitch
inside and out, had withstood
the *most* perfect storm.

And he sang:
A job well done
feels like re-ward time,
gonna let myself
be some-body.

○ Reincarnation

I'm coming back as a melody;
a noble thought/feeling/emotion
to give birth to me
a clear soft Fitzgerald's note
in Ella's throat high and afar,
a whole note trebling on.
I will come down on a Mills Brothers' bass,
slow, deep, heavy.
As an incarnation of Miles' prince
I'll transpose myself into three-quarter time,
and come down on down
to the earthy, bluesy, sensuous level
where Bessie, Billie, Vaughn and McRae
will stretch me out,
entwining my limbs around sixteen bars.
I'll swing away with obvious ease
monkeying around in the aura of Thelonius
touching on all levels.
I'll make riffs chased by Ellington classical fingers
keeping my rhythm with the untold talents
of immortal Steveland.
When I tire of gliding through octaves,
I'll level off to that one note
held in Louie's horn
where I'll skip on and on with MJQ
in scat bop style through time, yes,
I'm coming back as a melody.

○ Deja Vu

Like a yellow flag, my mind plants
a signpost for itself, a re-vision

of something I've never seen, the re-seeing
of a scene I never wrote. Here it is again,
Soweto. Women walking on a road. Bodies
shaped in angles that hold a three-sided

fury with gnarled hair; slender shadows
whose reappearance could give me the chance
to rewrite my descriptive passages of the corpses
they bear, the blood they wring from their skirts.

As if clairvoyance were a gift, I've been given
the second sight of girls, boys, silhouetted
against a casaba moon, slipping past a gatekeeper
into cliché: thousands dead or missing.

And living *is* a sending out of moments. That
is the gift. Each must come back in deja vu
like a pod on a bough of the akee-fruit tree,
opening in its time, round with delight or venom.

Photograph by Leigh H. Mosley

Maxine Clair is a native of Kansas. She has degrees from the University of Kansas, and The American University in Washington, D.C. Her work has appeared in many magazines, including the *Washington Review of the Arts, Obsidian,* and *Gargoyle.*